ANIMALS with LO[...]

Created by
Peter M. Spizzirri

Copyright, ©, 1996 by Spizzirri Publishing, Inc., All rights reserved.

This Is An Educational FACTS AND FUN Book of ANIMALS with LONG NECKS • Published by SPIZZIRRI PUBLISHING, INC., P.O. BOX 9397, RAPID CITY, SOUTH DAKOTA 57709. No part of this publication may be reproduced, stored in a retrievable system, or transmitted in any form without the express written consent of the publisher. All national and international rights reserved on the entire contents of this publication.
Printed in U.S.A.

OKAPI
Okapia johnstoni

If you want to see an okapi, you will have to look very hard. It loves to be alone and is nocturnal (comes out at night). That is why no one even knew it existed until 1971. It eats fruit and leaves that grow in the rain forest of Zaire, Africa.

• •

An okapi's neck can be 22 inches long.

OKAPI
Okapia johnstoni

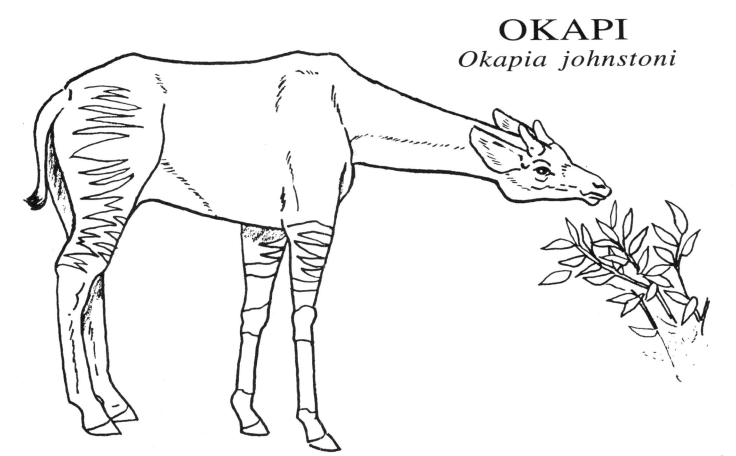

FLAMINGO

Phoenicopterus ruber

Flamingos can grow to be 6 feet tall. They are beautiful to watch as they fly, extending their necks and legs and spreading their wings to span 70 inches. Their trumpeting and honking can be heard as they call to one another while gliding gracefully on air currents.

• •

A flamingos neck can be 2 feet long.

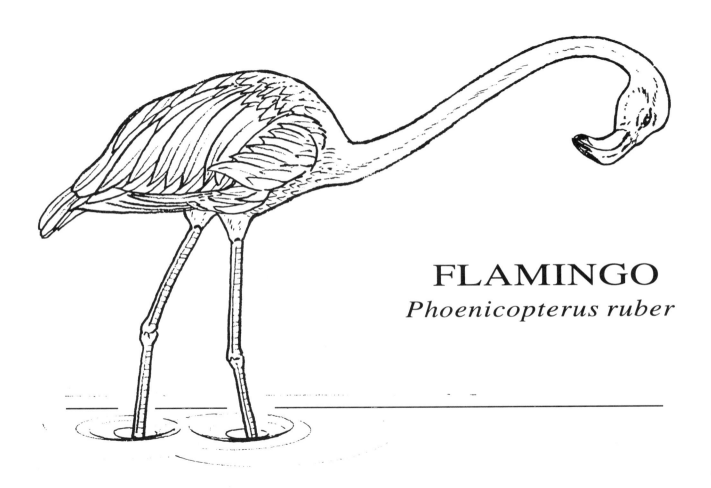

FLAMINGO
Phoenicopterus ruber

CAMEL
Camelus dromedarius

From North Africa to India, the domestic one hump Arabian camel is bred as a beast of burden, or a riding camel. It can trot at 10 miles per hour from 75 to 120 miles a day. No other animal can withstand the desert heat and travel so far on practically no food or water.

• •

A camel's neck is about 2 feet long.

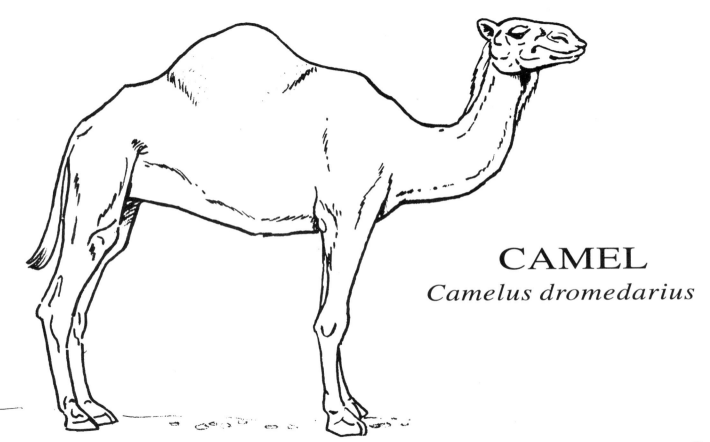

CAMEL

Camelus dromedarius

OSTRICH
Phoenicopterus ruber

Even though the 8 foot tall ostrich cannot fly, it is not at a disadvantage. It can run, taking 10 foot strides, at 40 miles per hour. The ostrich is starting to be raised domestically for food. It tastes much like beef but is lower in cholesterol.

. . . .

The ostrich has a 3 feet long neck.

OSTRICH
Phoenicopterus ruber

DIBATAG
Ammodorcas clarkei

A dibatag lives among the thorn trees in the dry sandy region of Somaliland. Its slender body has long legs (measuring 67 inches) and tiny hoofs. They blend right in with the vegetation, so, they cannot be seen when they are standing still.

• •

This dibatag has a 18 inch long neck.

DIBATAG
Ammodorcas clarkei

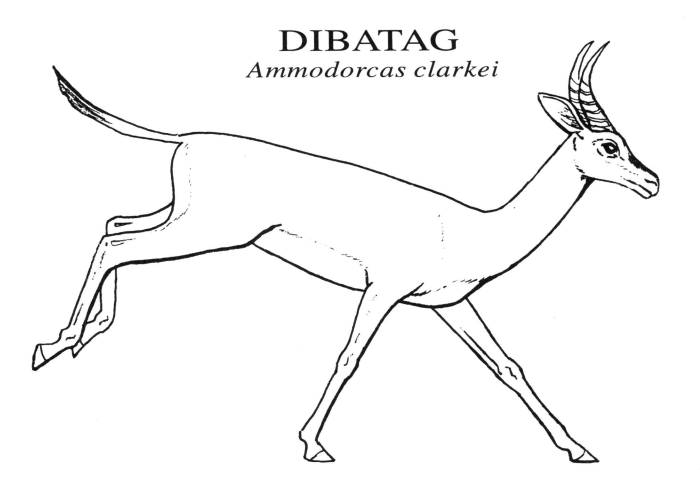

GIRAFFE
Giraffa camelopardalis

The tallest land mammal in the world is the giraffe. Growing to 19 feet, their large size stops them from lying down. They stand even while sleeping. It sure is funny to see them drinking ....it looks like they're trying to do the splits!

● ●

A giraffe's neck can be 7 feet long.

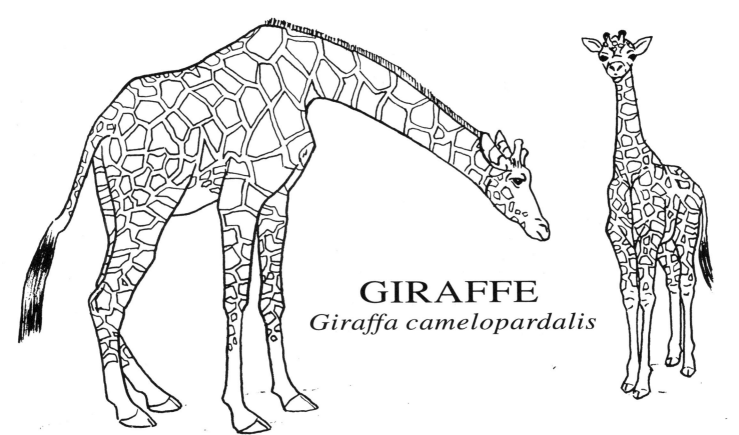

GIRAFFE
Giraffa camelopardalis

SNAKE-NECKED TURTLE
Chelodina longicollis

This small turtle has a five inch shell. What is interesting is that its neck is as long as its shell. Few animals have necks almost as long as their bodies. This long neck allows them rest in shallow waters and not be seen, while they have their nose above water to breath.

• •

This turtle's neck is as long as its shell.

SNAKE-NECKED TURTLE
Chelodina longicollis

GREAT BLUE HERON
Ardea herodias

The great blue heron is able to stand absolutely motionless while waiting to spear a fish for dinner. Can you stand as still as a statue? It's unusual that this bulky 4 foot long bird, is able to float and take flight from the water (like a duck does). Most wading birds can't do that!

• •

This heron's neck is 18 inches long.

GREAT BLUE HERON
Ardea herodias

GUANACO
Lama guanacoe

South America's largest land mammal depends on speed and alertness to keep it safe. When frightened, it can run at speeds up to 35 miles per hour (56km). Guanacos live in small herds with one male as the leader and protector. A domestic guanaco is called a llama.

• •

The guanaco has a neck 18 inches long.

GUANACO
Lama guanacoe

19

MUTE SWAN
Cygnus olor

Do you know where Europe is on the world map? That is where the mute swan comes from. It was brought across the ocean to America. This lovely bird got its name from the muted humming sound that is made, by the flapping of its wings, while in flight.

• •

The mute swan's neck is 18 inches long.

MUTE SWAN
Cygnus olor

21

GERENUK
Litocranius walleri

Gerenuk are at home in dry thornbush country of Africa. They eat plants and leaves. All the water they need to live is in the food they eat. When they want to reach leaves high on bushes, they stand on their hind legs. This enables them to reach heights of 7 feet.

• •

The gerenuk has a 24 inch long neck.

GERENUK
Litocranius walleri

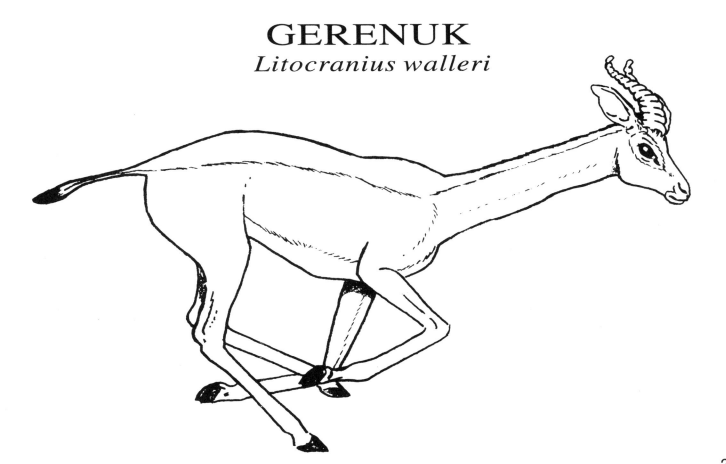

OTHER CHILDREN'S BOOKS CREATED BY SPIZZIRRI PUBLISHING

ISBN (INTERNATIONAL STANDARD BOOK NUMBER) PREFIX ON ALL SPIZZIRRI BOOKS IS: 0-86545-

EDUCATIONAL READ AND COLOR BOOKS

ILLUSTRATIONS AND TEXT
SIZE: 8 1/2" X 11"

AIRCRAFT
ANIMAL ALPHABET
ANIMAL F. CALENDAR
ANIMAL GIANTS
ATLANTIC FISH
AUTOMOBILES
BIRDS
CALIFORNIA INDIANS
CALIFORNIA MISSIONS
CATS
CATS OF THE WILD
CAVE MAN
COLONIES
COMETS
Count/Color DINOSAURS
COWBOYS
DEEP-SEA FISH
DINOSAURS
DINOSAURS OF PREY
DOGS
DOGS OF THE WILD
DOLLS
DOLPHINS
EAGLES
ENDANGERED BIRDS
Endang'd Mam'ls-AFRICA

Endang'd Mam'ls- ASIA & CHINA
Endang'd Mam'ls-SO. AMERICA
ENDANGERED SPECIES
ESKIMOS
FARM ANIMALS
FISH
HORSES
KACHINA DOLLS
LAUTREC POSTERS
MAMMALS
MARINE MAMMALS
MARSUPIALS
NORTHEAST INDIANS
NORTHWEST INDIANS
PACIFIC FISH
PALEOZOIC LIFE
PENGUINS
PICTURE CROSSWORDS
PICTURE DICTIONARY
PIONEERS
PLAINS INDIANS
PLANETS
POISONOUS SNAKES
Prehist. BIRDS
Prehist. FISH
Prehist. MAMMALS
Prehist. SEA LIFE
PRIMATES

RAIN FOREST BIRDS
RAIN FOREST RIVER LIFE
RAIN FOREST TREE LIFE
REPTILES
ROCKETS
SATELLITES
SHARKS
SHIPS
SHUTTLE CRAFT
SOUTHEAST INDIANS
SOUTHWEST INDIANS
SPACE CRAFT
SPACE EXPLORERS
STATE BIRDS
STATE FLOWERS
TEXAS
TRANSPORTATION
TRUCKS
WHALES

SILHOUETTE ART BOOKS
8 1/2 x 11" Reproducible

CHRISTMAS
CIRCUS
DINOSAURS
FARM ANIMALS
OCEAN LIFE
ZOO ANIMALS

EDUCATIONAL ACTIVITY BOOKS
SIZE: 5 1/2 x 8 1/2"

Alphabet Dot-to-dot **PETS**
Alphabet Dot-to-dot **ZOO ANIMALS**
BIRD MAZES
BUTTERFLY MAZES
DINOSAUR MAZES
Dot-to-dot DINOSAURS
Dot-to-dot FISH
Dot-to-dot REPTILES
Dot-to-dot WHALES
FARM MAZES
FISH MAZES
FLOWER MAZES
MAMMAL MAZES
SHARK MAZES
SHELL MAZES
TREE MAZES
TURTLE MAZES
ZOO MAZES

Educational FACTS and FUN Books
SIZE: 5 1/2 X 8 1/2"

ANIMAL LEAPS
ANIMAL SPEEDS
ANIMALS THAT LAY EGGS
ANIMALS WITH LONG NECKS
ANIMALS WITH LONG TAILS
BIRD SPEEDS

FOOTPRINTS OF BIRDS
INSECT HUNTERS
MAMMAL FOOTPRINTS
POISONOUS ANIMALS
SKATES AND RAYS
SMALL MAMMALS

EARLY LEARNING WORKBOOKS
SIZE: 8 1/2 x 11"

ALPHABET PICTURES
COMPLETE THE WORDS
COUNTING DINOSAURS
Dot to dot ALPHABET
Dot to dot NUMBERS
FIRST ADDITION
FIRST ALPHABET
FIRST NUMBERS
FIRST SUBTRACTION
MAKE A CALENDAR
MAKING WORDS
MAZE PUZZLES
NUMBERS and COLORS
PICTURE CROSSWORDS
PICTURE DICTIONARY
SHAPES, ART & COLORS
THEY GO TOGETHER
TRIANGLE PICTURES
WORD HUNT PUZZLES
WORDS IN WORDS